Testimonial

As it has been stated by many, "We are Spiritual beings having a physical experience". I am honoured to have come to know Brenda. Although through a painful physical experience, it has become not her Breakdown, but her Breakthrough!

You will read, then feel in these beautiful and honest poems, the highs and lows; the ebbs and flows; the confidences and fears and the true Bliss that can be experienced through the Divine.

~ Nicole Dunn

~~~

Do You Believe?

~~~

A story of my spiritual transformation
and healing in a collection of poems
and stories.

~~~

Do You Believe?

Written by Brenda Jeppesen

Copyright 2011 Brenda Jeppesen

Jeppesen Edition, Dec 2011

ISBN: 978-0-9879026-2-7

~~

~~ As a seed we are planted here on Earth, to adapt and grow - our rebirth. With each new day, as we embrace the universal energies, you will see this seed transform to be - one of life's beauties! ~~

~~

Table of Contents

Gratitude

I am grateful to all whom have come into my life, to the ones who have yet to come into my life, to all the readers who had the courage to believe and especially to my guide and friend, Nicole for seeing the light within me! Without your support and enlightenment this book would not have been possible.

Foreward

I am reminded of a quote by K.T. Long, "It is only when we silent the blaring sound of our daily existence that we can finally hear the whispers of truth that life reveals to us, as it stands knocking on the doorsteps of our hearts." This sentiment strongly resonates with me as my Life Journey continues to affirm the substance of this adage more and more each day.

I had the opportunity in 2009 to attend a workshop called "emPOWERed Women" there we were asked to come up with a mantra. After a few moments of thought, I came up with "If you have the desire; you have the power!" I remember this quote ignited something [a force, a power] within me and for some time, nothing could stop me. Well, that's not completely true because in late 2009 my body stopped me to the point where it appeared there was no return but thankfully a transformation happened in 2010 which lead me to a journey of spiritual and personal transformation. This book of poems documents my thoughts, feelings and events over a 6 week period of that transformation. I continue on this journey and today, if you were to ask me what my mantra is, I would simply say "Be your authentic self."

Growing up in the swinging sixties in a non-religious home, raised by two loving parents who sheltered me from the chaos of the world, I would best describe myself as a NERD. I didn't really know there was an authentic self to me back then. As I look back today, what I believe made me different from most was that I lived in the "now". At each moment of every day, I would take in all the beauty around me. Whether I was lying in a field of clover using my senses to see, hear, feel, smell and vibrate with everything around me, or whether it was becoming one with something as intricate as a computer – analyzing how it worked or the code that orchestrated its function, I was always present in the moment and experienced everything to the fullest. Further, I was a highly sensitive child, although no family member was aware (until now that is - LOL), I was frequently visited by my deceased grandmother. Yup, there it is. I saw my father's mother first when I fell down the basement stairs. There she was, about 4 feet in front of me looking right at me. It was as if the cold concrete wall of the basement had opened up this time warp tunnel and my grandmother appeared washing calmness and a love over me. It happened again a few times in early adulthood, usually during highly stressful times. Can you say guardian angel? That's what she was to me, never speaking, but always giving me the sense of being loved and protected. Her presence made me feel different made me feel special. It wasn't something I broadcasted to friends or family. No one ever approached me saying they just saw our deceased Uncle Bob (ha-ha) so why would I run around doing the same? Something inside of me always told me that this wasn't what everyone experienced. I was never afraid of this and never believed anything was wrong with me. In fact, I always felt a part of a secret society in which I was the only member – which was okay with me since I was an introvert anyways! I loved being alone with myself so I continued through my entire life with a buttoned upper lip and not sharing my experiences with anyone that was until my transformation.

During my transformation I had many ahaa moments. One in particular was when I tried to come to terms with why I had such a hard time embracing love. As I recalled, in my pre-teens, my maternal grandmother took me on vacation with her to Italy. There, I learned a hard lesson, that adults can be cruel. I have always loved wholly and open heartedly yet this experience caused me to believe I could be extreme in showing my love. On that trip, I was told I should tone down my "extreme" expression of love. I was instantly confused to be told such a thing, in Italy of all places, a place where it was a normal practice for men to show their admiration by driving by and pinching you. Why was I getting in trouble for showing affection to my relatives – why was giving too many hugs a bad thing? Hmm.

This burden of a "lesson" stayed with me as I grew into adulthood. I learnt it was better to quiet my voice and keep secrets as to what I wanted and restrain the love I felt from others. It was ok for me to show them some of me, but very much of me was hidden. Even though I have had a fairly successful career, my relationship radar had sucked as most of my partnerships where abusive in nature. There was little old me, holding everything in, keeping more secrets and never really revealing what I wanted or needed. I gave my love freely and never got much in return or took much in return, it's what I had been conditioned to do, I understand that now. Even though I always managed to sport a smile on my face, I was filled with sadness, darkness and hope, all at the same time. I always knew there was more, something greater and that I existed for a purpose, to me this was the thing that most resonated within me.

It wasn't until recently in 2010 when I started to make sense of all the connections between what I was experiencing as a child spiritually and emotionally and how it related to my perceptions today, how it was holding me back from embracing abundance in my life. One of the biggest ahaa moments was when I determined I was selling myself short and have been for most of my life but it took a major life event to wake me up!

It started on December 31, 2009 when I lost something very dear to me – my back. Yes, my back, you know the spine in the lumbar area that holds us up and allows us to walk straight each day with a sense of pride. All of a sudden, I was unable to work or provide the full level of care to my disabled spouse. At times, simple tasks, such as going to the washroom seemed like a near impossible task. While imposed by chronic bed rest for the first month of 2010, I visited the emergency room many times with little to no relief. A MRI showed that I had significant issues with the majority of my lower vertebrae. The prescribed medications proved to be ineffective. I spent four days of each week over a five month period seeking every type of conventional therapy that was available including, cold laser therapy, traction, physiotherapy, IFC, TENS and massage therapy to name a few. Each promising that I would be better in three months.

6 months later, still in considerable pain and unhealed, I insisted that I be allowed to return to work. I had responsibilities after all, and it was time for me to get back to real life. I pushed myself and returned on a graduated hour's schedule against doctors' advice. But at that point in my life, staying home was not healing me; I needed to try to return to reality. The hour and a half commute was exhausting, the three and a half hour day that I spent in my office felt like a week. But I was determined to make it work. To my dismay, my return to work lasted only two weeks, at which point I suffered a major setback. The doctors advised me that I may never be able to work again. I was absolutely devastated! However, as I sit here today, having returned to work fulltime, I realize that the doctor's prognosis was the catalyst that resulted in a life altering change for me

because at that point, the universe spoke, and it chose to speak loudly since I obviously hadn't been listening.

The very next day, I was introduced to Nicole Dunn, an acupuncturist and holistic healer. During my first visit with Nicole, she administered the Bowen Technique as well as some Reiki. This was my first experience with both of these modalities. At the end of the session, I clearly remember skipping out, laughing, free of the pain that had been plaguing me for several months, filled with hope and a feeling of overwhelming joy. I decided to pursue these therapy sessions with Nicole on a weekly basis for 6-8 weeks. During those subsequent visits, I incorporated meditation, a well-practiced technique for me, but had recently neglected due to the pain that I was experiencing. I have to laugh at this as I write this because the one thing that was so important to do for me during this challenging time was to meditate and yet it was the one thing I had ignored.

The year leading up to my back giving out, I had been experiencing some interesting visions during my meditations. With my eyes closed, I could see beautiful purple colors swirling around emitting pure bliss. During my Bowen sessions, the visions became stronger, appearing as circular bands, which at times seem to be expanding and moving away while at other times, seem to become smaller and closing in towards me. As time passed, lightening bright white stars would appear, giving me the feeling that I was travelling through space. Then I started to see a bright white lightening orb in the centre of my field of vision. It would appear and diminish several times during the session. After each session, I would emerge feeling overwhelmingly calm, energized and loved beyond words. I then decided to pursue weekly sessions with Bowen and meditation.

As the sessions progressed, Nicole was able to guide me with absolute grace in all I didn't know. Everything started to make sense, my thoughts, happenings including my childhood experiences [even those in Italy]. I started reading up on the mind-body connection, the power of "now" and who I really AM [books by Carolyn Myss, Eckhart Tolle, Deepak Chopra to name a few]. I found myself beginning to trust my own intuition, to understand and recognise the Divine in me and others – learning we are all one. It wasn't easy. It involved taking a hard look within and analyzing my thoughts to gain insight into what lay deep within. At times, it felt like insight had slapped me on the side of my face as I realized some things with such overwhelming clarity.

During this time, strange events started to occur: unexplained bruising, body sensations, shaking/trembling, visions and what appeared to be signs started to pop up all around me

My dreams became magical -- almost as if they were real (hard to explain). They were clearly telling me I was awakening spiritually. One dream in particular introduced me to the crystal Celestine. Little did I know that the Angel in my dream was giving me clear indication on what I needed to work on. After much analysis which included learning about the different Angels, it became obvious I had been visited by Angel Celestina and I needed to work on my 5th chakra and self-expression. A transformation was happening and honestly...it felt a bit like a roller coaster ride. Some of my days were filled with bliss, others were filled with despair, and many were filled with questions. To the outside world I am sure that it appeared that I was losing my mind (some days I thought I might be). Thankfully I was able to share my thoughts and experiences with some close friends without the fear of being judged. I now know that I am blessed (we are all blessed); we just need to open our eyes, open our hearts and believe.

In the midst of this transformation I started to write poems which if you really knew me, you would find strange. English had never been one of my favourite subjects in school; I was more drawn to the maths and sciences. During my session one week with Nicole, I mentioned how poems seemed to be flowing out of me and the strange thing was I have never really written a poem before but it was like something needed to come out, something stronger than will, something deep within was erupting and it was as if my thoughts had been consumed with rhyme and my hand consumed with pen and paper. That's when the discussion of channelling surfaced and on June 10th I pulled out my trusty dowsing rods which had recently become my go to tool to the Divine answers within. The most obvious burning question was "Are these poems being channelled?", the answer I received was a very strong yes. As the excitement built within me I paused and wrote down a few more burning questions in order to keep my thoughts clear. I started to ask what each letter of their name was. As I made my way through the alphabet my dousing rods confirmed it was

St. Jude. I have to admit that I didn't know who St. Jude was so I ventured to the internet to do some research. I have to admit I was a little taken back when I read St. Jude was the patron saint of hopeless causes and lost cases. Was I the lost cause? My heart dropped. I ran to my dousing rods again to ask was I the lost cause. The answer I got was no. I continued to ask why, when , how many poems and well, the rest is history. A history that is now in print for me to share with you, the universe and documented in the collection of these poems.

As I continue along my Journey, my daily challenge is to learn, pray and be grateful for all that I have, what we all have. In this chaotic world of ours, one of my greatest challenges is maintaining silence within. The "committee" in my head seems to work overtime some days. While I love them dearly, I've decided it's finally time to take them off the payroll and move on but that's easier said than done. To the idle observer, my life today probably very much mirrors the past. I still have the high stress job; I am still the primary caregiver for my spouse. However, I have now incorporated many holistic modalities into my life. I take time for me. I meditate. I pray. Most importantly

I perceive things differently. Healing is very challenging and does not happen overnight; however I know that I am on the right path, it feels right. My misfortune was the catalyst that opened my mind's eye and me to this awakening! I am so grateful for many things. A quote comes to mind by Cynthia Ozick – "We often take for granted the very things that most deserve our gratitude". For most of us, this is so true in our everyday lives. As a result of my journey over the past year, I am grateful every day. I am grateful for the experiences/challenges that have presented themselves over the past 16 months, the friends and family I have in this life, my guide, my teacher, my friend Nicole, and most of all the Divine in me!

I AM now on a Journey of self-discovery and unconditional love and I wouldn't change a thing!

So you may be asking yourself why I felt the need to share my pain, joy, and blissful delight with the world in these pages you are about to read. Well, other than the fact that my life has been touched by the Divine and these poems were channelled through me with the guidance of St. Jude, I feel an overwhelming drive to pay it forward. Truly, it is my hope that something resonates with you. If there is one thing that I have realized it's that we are all the same. Yes we all have our own stories, our own history that has conditioned us to be who we are today, yes we look different, we act differently; but if you pull away all the layers, we are all one. It is my hope that you will see that I could be you (you could be me), you too could wake up one day and realize that you have been touched by the Divine. Throughout my lifetime I would have never imagined that this could've been possible. If someone had told me this "creative" connection to the Divine could happen, I probably would have been a little sceptical. If it can happen to me, then it can happen to you of course since we are all connected – all one. I would wish for nothing more for you! Trust me it's not a ticket to easy street but it is a ticket to inner peace, that is, if you are willing to look deep within, face the truths and believe!

I know you have it in you; you are a beautiful spiritual being capable of amazing things. You are not alone; you are part of this greater energy, part of me, part of the All!

Enjoy!

My Secret Love

With each breath I see you more clearly now

Like a baby, I am comforted in your warm
strong embrace

A Divine golden braid caresses and engulfs
my heart

I can feel your heart beat as it melts with
mine

With the warmth of your being, my spirit
lifts

My breath calms - cleansing me of my fear
and pain

My existence is one and my eyes flood with
gratitude

I am lost in the ocean of bliss - chaos
drowned by silence

I cry out for help

It's as if you cradle me and place a warm
breast of milk across my lips

A love and light flows over my tongue into
the core of my being

Like an ocean of love, I AM submerged

Every cell in my body is ignited, lost in a world so full of energy and love

This is beyond what I've ever known. I feel you, I feel me, and we are whole

I AM

Namaste!

Another Answer Came!

The first day I met you
I was in so much pain
Life as I knew
Would never be the same

After feeling your grace
I was filled with hope
This was the place
Time for me to grab the rope

Another answer came
As you guided me to see
This was all a game
I needed to just be

With each moment with you
I learned to be
To listen to my body

And become more of me

You gave me the love I needed

I wanted I craved

You helped me see the truth

The whole new day

Another answer came

As you guided me to see

This was all a game

I needed to just be

I gained insight and wisdom

But when I finally believed

A flood more questions

The answers received

Like the warm sun on my face

Feeling loved and whole

I ask for nothing now

Except what is my role?

Another answer came

As you guided me to see

This was all a game

I just needed to be me

Every Time I See You

Every time I see you
I realize who I AM
Every time I feel you
I believe I can

When I feel your touch
A Divine love flows through my veins
Ignites my soul
And lights my way

Every time I see you
I realize who I AM
Anything is possible
I know who I AM

I AM beauty
I AM love and
I AM full of grace

When I first met you
I didn't know your name
Your long flowing hair
Transformed me into an angelic daze

I have come to love you
A love beyond this realm
When you first came to see me
The dream that made me delve

Offering your guidance
In unspoken words
Floating in your presence
My new found urge

Every time I see you
I realize who I AM
Anything is possible
I know who I AM

I AM beauty

I AM love and
I AM full of grace

You gave me a voice
One that can express my creative ways
It gave me strength
To see the way

All I know now
Is this is love and light
I want to be with you
Morning, noon and night

Every time I see you
I realize who I AM
Anything is possible
I know who I AM

I AM beauty
I AM love and
I AM full of grace

Love Is The Answer

Girl I can see it in your eyes
There is a love that you desire
You gave your love so freely
But they knocked you down tired
You learnt to give and not receive
I need you to believe

Girl you can shine, it's your time.
Love is the answer
Don't you want to know?
Know how it feels
When love flows

You think you don't deserve it
Because of what they told you as a babe
Close your eyes and feel
You need to understand that love can be real

Take my hand
Come closer, its ok
It is as it should be
I'll show you the way

Girl you can shine, it's your time
Love is the answer
Don't you want to know?
Know how it feels
When love flows

I'll show you what you need
And what I know is true
Your energy will be on fire
It's what you have always desired

Don't you understand?
That when you do
It makes us all complete
The sum not two

Complete to be
Who we truly are
And share our special gifts
In this Eden of breath

Girl you can shine, it's your time
Love is the answer
Don't you want to know?
Know how it feels
When this Divine love flows

Come, let's get intoxicated
In the mystical thing called love
Girl you deserve it... the answer is love

Take You On A Ride

Just imagine if you let me take you on a ride

Dissolving all attachments to what might be, you will feel so alive

Through snow sleet rain and drought

Let me take away your fears and doubt

We can see the universe

At the speed of light

You're not flying solo

You'll know its right

You have the tools to travel the road right in front of you

Many others have succeeded too

Balance is key

Dressed with knowledge, wisdom and the freedom to be

You just have to get on the ride

There is no time for pride

With your feet planted firmly on the ground,
grab hold tight

Butterflies will take flight

Holding trust and forgiveness in your hands

Rev it up to untouched lands

Your heart starts racing

Let it be - like the birds and the bees

Surrender – be one, believe

Call upon the spirit of thee

As momentum builds, moments enrich

I will shield you from the ditch

Sun, moon and fire

Replaced by your inner most desires

Just imagine if you let me take you on a ride

Dissolving all attachments to what might be,
you will feel so alive

Through snow sleet rain and drought

Let me take away your fears and doubt

We can see the universe

At the speed of light

You're not flying solo

You'll know it's right

Feel the wind in your hair

Angels they appear

Bright fire of truth, no word of time

You are all mine

Every second counts

Throw away your doubts

My ride is beyond expectation

It will blow your imagination

Just imagine if you let me take you on a ride

Dissolving all attachments to what might be,
you will feel so alive

Through snow sleet rain and drought

Let me take away your fears and doubt

We can see the universe
At the speed of light
You're not flying solo
You'll know it's right

Ode To O

Come on... Dive in and let your mind go

Delve deep in the ocean and discover all the treasures below

Yet to be uncovered; yet to be your lover

You are light; you are love – all you need is O, it's a drug like no other

Once you discover; you won't want to let go

The journey is boundless; keep your eye on the gold

It's a Divine drug this thing called O

Can you break the coooode?

It was first discovered in 1774

Its atomic number is 8 for those in the know

It's the third most abundant element in the sun and Mother Earth

You can even find it at birth

Nine tenths of the mass of water; two thirds
of our form

It's colourless, odourless and tasteless; yet it
livens all which is born

Your cells need it to turn food to fuel

But be careful this drug, it can be cruel

No need to line up, it doesn't discriminate
young or old

Rich or poor it's the only Divine drug out
there not sold

Yet to be uncovered; yet to be your lover

You are light; you are love – all you need is
O, it's a drug like no other

Once you discover; you won't want to let go

The journey is boundless; keep your eye on
the gold

Don't you know it's the new drug of this
millennium?

It's a necessary component to open up your
planetarium

Breath deep, dive in, it a Divine drug this thing called O

Once you discover; you won't want to let go

Oxygen!

If I Never

If I never found you
I wonder- would I have found me?
When I'm around you
The world is filled with such possibilities

Now living every moment
In this cosmic bliss
Each day so rich
How can one be so blessed?

It seems irrational at times
It doesn't even cost a dime
How can it be so sublime?
I've never known anything so Divine

I now dance in the rain
Washing away the shame and fear
I open myself up
As there is no pretending here

Following a sense which steers

I fall to my knees

Saying how can you love me?

Can it really be?

Each time we are near

There is a oneness unexplained

I love the light that washes over my body

And courses through my veins

A calmness and excitement fills each empty space

No sense trying to hide as it's written all over my face

At times I faultered and you picked me right back up

You challenge me, you love me, you show me all the beauty uncut

At times I feel obsessed

At times I couldn't care less

You tell me things about me

That I don't even see

At that moment in time it makes it so easy to
embrace love over fear

Certainty over doubt and breathe

I often wonder would I have found me

If I never found you it would be hard to see

Every Time I Feel You Cry

Every time I feel you cry
My thoughts race
My heart beat ups its pace
My shields come up
My wings envelope

Don't cry baby; all will be ok
Change the subject, make a joke
All will go away

As my eyes start to dry
I ask why can't I cry?
It will release, what's hidden inside
But there it resides

Every time I feel you cry
I want to hid
Oh baby don't cry
Just hide it on the other side

You Fill Me - It Has Me Believing

I know you see right through me
I cannot hide my internal speech
You see my strengths and weaknesses
And you still love me

Burning in me is a desire
You are all I require
Each day I make time to be with you
Each night I go to sleep thinking of you

When I'm with you nothing else exists
I only want this feeling to persist
You fill every cell of my being
It has me believing

How Come It's Only You Who Sees?

How come it is only you who sees?
When I try to share part of me
The people in my life don't care to see

I offer to share my poems
The answer is why
It doesn't feel like home
Why do I even try?

I send them to you
And you send loving comments back
That I would hope I would receive
From the people I thought believed

Am I living an illusion to what really is?
Should I accept it or say I am hurt?
Why bother as I revert.

How come it is only you who sees?

It is because you are on a different
frequency?

Now I share in silence

Trying to find balance

I'm sorry if I'm flooding you with these

But it gives me comfort when someone
believes

I want to run from these needy ways

But for now it saves my day

Oh Beloved

Oh beloved you bring me such glee

Sending out an abundance of love and light
for all to see

Others have yet to uncover what you mean
to me

I marvel at your beauty as I cradle your
wondrous sappy lips

I am transformed by this thing called bliss

In the morning all covered in dew

I am grateful to see your form anew

As you open your lush mystical wings
soaking up the sun beams

I get lost in the mischievous beauty of one it
seems

Up close I relish your sweet scent as you tip
your fragrance to the air

I and passerbys are enchanted beyond repair

Your pools of lace so delicate, so soft

You prisms of white and pink, I get lost

It's no wonder your regal beauty irresistible
to some

China, Japan and other king-doms

Oh beloved have no shame

Your bashfulness nature is but a game

Named after Paeon, the Greek god of
medicine and healing

It's no wonder your blossoms are so
revealing

Made of riches and honour you stand so
erect

If I nurture you along a stick

Known for your large, showy ways

You continue to hold me in your daze

Oh Beloved, I am transformed by this thing
called bliss

In the depths of your soul, earthy
purifications

Some cultivate your roots for the cure of
afflictions

In the midst of night, the evening dew
intensifies your scent

Beloved I get swept away with your
fragrance and color

You are like no other

Oh beloved you bring me such glee

Sending out an abundance of love and light
for all to see

Others have yet to uncover what you mean
to me

My beloved bloom Peonies

I have been mesmerized by you

How you love this world my beloved bloom

You Gotta Listen!

You gotta listen to your body
Gotta listen to your self
Don't listen to just anybody
Unless they know oneself

Look deep within for answers
To find who you truly are
It's the only door to freedom
You are a star

Your purpose yet to discover
All the glory you can be
It's time to get a life
One that can set you free

You gotta listen to your body
Gotta listen to your self
Don't listen to just anybody
Unless they know oneself

Manifested thru your talents
They are never far from you
That thing you do so easily
Is the way to be true to you

You must sit quiet and listen to yourself
Reflect on your whole life
And ask yourself
What is it, I do right?

The answer is within you
It's only you who can see the light
Don't question truth
For it is right

You gotta listen to your body
Gotta listen to your self
Don't listen to just anybody
Unless they know oneself

The purpose in your life

Will set you free
It will let you be
All you can be

The boundaries are limitless
Do you see?
Listen deep within you
For all you can be

Message To Me

Today I struggle
Consumed with doubt
Someone please tell me the answers
What is my life all about?

I question but I know
What is really true
It's silly but we question
That which we are here to do

The answers lie within me
I have to believe
And follow the clues
To see what I can be

If I get it wrong, it simply means
I have to go back in me
Nothing worth having is ever free
But this time that's ok, it's for me

It Will Be As It Should Be

Never have I picked up a pen

To write a poem before

Yet these past few weeks

They have been pouring out of me, so much
that I cannot ignore

A friend of mine suggested it may be
channelling

So I ask my rod for guidance for my higher
good

And it confirms the messages

Are from St. Jue

I Google my findings and I see

Saint Jude, the patron saint of Jesus

So I ask my rod is this whom it could be?

And my rod confirms with certainty

Excited by the prospect

I start to read

What is St. Jude trying to tell me?

The Saint of hopeless cases and lost causes
Is it me they talk about?
I can't believe – so I ask my dowsing rod
And it tells me something very odd

I am to write 70 poems that channel thru me
And publish them for the world to see

I then ask "Why me?"
And the reply I get
Is because you see

Overwhelmed by this message
I start to cry
Oh Thank You, Thank You, Thank You
Spirit guides

I want to ask more questions
But I know if I just believe
It will be; as it should be

Touch

I haven't been myself lately
Feeling kinda blue
It seems all I needed
Was a touch of you

Like kids in a playground
Running, laughing, free
One can fall and scrap their knee

But when someone comes over
And simply touches them
All that seemed so wrong
Is well again

Last night I was touched by an angel
An angel who lent their hand
Within minutes
I knew who I was again

On the dark days

When you can hardly see

Remember to be gentle

And accept someone's grace – believe.

Come With Me

Your body filled with pain
Your body filled with fear
Can't you see all I want
Is for you to be here

In a place filled with love
A place so special from above
If you could only see
You would know how special you are to me

You see when you hurt
It hurts me too
We all must show our light
To help in the universal plight

It's magical you'll see
It's where we all need to be
So calm yourself and breath
Come with me to this unknown galaxy

Don't Know What To Do

With each cruel word my energy is spent
How can I ever repair this dent?
Do I stay and falsely repent?
Or should I run off to a convent?

The problem you see is
I don't know what to do
Will I be lost without you?
Oh teacher please tell me
What it is I need to see?

I feel I don't know how to find me
Is this a test that I must stay?
In hopes to find me another day
All I know is I'm so much happier in the
presence of thee

Only the fear to leave
Prevents me from finding me

The Child Within

As a child quiet and introverted
You hid behind the pant leg of your father
Shy - holding back the real you

Thoughts were deep
Whether it was real or not
Everything analyzed
Every answer sought

Comforted in your inner world
No one had to know
You were crying out for love
Love that would not grow

As you grew
You continued to learn
It was easier to give
But expectations continued to hurt the child
within

Oddly enough
When you got unconditional love
You shawn like a beacon briefly
But you continued to shove

It energized your spirit
Until someone wanted in
You would close the door
Considering it a sin

Words of kindness so genuine
Would make you shiver and grin
Blocking the love
Saying no one gets in

In order to grow
You must know
We are all children
Children within

You deserve
We all do

This thing you call sin

Let me help you come in
Come into the light
Leaving darkness behind
Don't be blind

We are all here for a reason
A reason to love
But it only works when
You hold the hand of love

Do You See?

As I walk by you
Do you see?
You are
That special part of me

We are one
The universal energies
That makes our lives
A mirror of thee

We are all born
With this gift to see
But we seem
To be sworn to secrecy

Our colors so bright
For all to see
Yet there are very few
Who use their gift to see

Someday I hope to be the one

That you walk by

And you see that you are me

It Was Meant To Be

I am asking you to see
It was meant to be
This thing that causes you goose bumps
And you deny

The world awaits your special gift
Yet you fill your time adrift
You must go do it now
Enormous is the crowd

Asking that you follow
And fulfill what you swallow
Don't hide anymore
Go swing that door

Go share your gift with others
You will discover
That it gives you peace
And makes the world complete

You Are Here

I love it when my body trembles
And when all colors appear
Not many can sense it
But I know you are here

I am reminded of your presence
As sweet smells filled with your essence
As wind blows across my face
I slow my pace

Walking through the gardens
Bees pollinating with such grace
It doesn't take a genius to stop and admire
this place

In the smile of a newborn
In the laughter of a child
In the simple things in life
I am reminded of you presence

When I reflect in the mirror
And finger my hair behind my ear
I am reminded of your presence
I know you are here

When I smell the scent of cinnamon
It ignites my soul
I am reminded of your presence
You are here

When I catch the eyes of a stranger
And feel a warm embrace
I am reminded of your presence
You are here

You exist in all there is
Everything and every place
I promise to share and love you
This thing called grace

I Have Yet To Meet You

People come into your life
To help you through the day
Others are meant to be there
To make you see the way

I have yet to meet you
But I know when we do
You will see that you were meant for me
As much as I for you

You might be the man that needs shelter
from the rain
On the day I most need it - you will tell me I
am sane
You might be a healer who helps me release
my pain
And I to you; might help you see your
efforts are not in vain

We each have a purpose
Many I'm sure

But when I meet you
Another will be cured

I have yet to meet you
And I know the day will come
When I can say it was a pleasure to meet
you
Another deed undone

Gut Instinct

When the moment comes you must take it
Otherwise you will remain the same
You can listen to your gut
To help you get thru this game

When things feel right
And you are filled with delight
Listen to your gut for the path is right

When you feel the heaviness
Senses unsure
Know this is the answer
This is a detour

There is no manual for
The tools that lay deep within
But you can read your body
And know where to begin

Gut instinct we call it

It's there for us to choose

We just need to recognize it

And have faith in the clues

What You Deserve

Dear friend you are so special to me
I want to see you happy

If I could choose
I would ask for you
Someone who during times of struggle
Comforts you

Someone who can see
All that you are
Someone who believes
Someone like me

I would ask that they love you
And show you the way
The way to our hearts
Each and everyday

They would hold you

And love you

But encourage you to go

To fulfil your dreams

Even if it meant postpone

I would ask that they support you

In your time of need

And on the good days

Just be

Someone to show you how special you are

Someone for you who has unconditional love

Someone who sees all that you are

Someone who believes

Someone like me

A spirit always there thru thick and thin

A spirit who appreciates the situation we are in

Someone who loves the simple things in life

Someone who adores you beyond your might

This is what I want for my special friend
Someone who sees your beauty within

The Lady Who Sees

You introduce me to a lady that sees

She asks me to rub my hands together in a downward vee

As she looks above my head - the aura she reads

She says to me it's not thyroid its sugars she heeds

She says there is anger but I must believe

Enjoy every moment no cause to bereav

Go home and play happy music

For the sceptics to hear

It will change the frequencies

It will help my dear

Enjoy every moment and let it just be

You have strong will and patience too

You will succeed

She tells me I give my love too freely

That I need to love me first, dearly

My new mantra she instructs is

I deserve love

As she continues to scan above

She then proceeds to say you will be fine

Just remember to embrace love, this is your lifeline.

I think to myself how to love me

One hasn't done so for an eternity

Is there a rule book that I need?

How does one change what they believe?

Look At Me

As I sit on my porch I look up to a tree and see

The morning sun peeking thru to me

I imagine what it would be like

To be this tree

Having love and light shined on me for free

Then I relish if I just be

My breath can take me to

The Divine in me

Having love and light shining out of me for free

Look at me I AM that tree

Oh Wondrous Tree

Oh wondrous old tree
Once started from seed
Nurtured by Mother Earth
Such large girth

Many a tales to tell
Generations under your spell
Enjoying your shelter
Splendid in your slumber

Your roots buried deep
To the mysteries below
The fruits we reap
As you continue to grow

Oh wondrous tree
We have so much to learn from thee

Your branches reach out
To the glory above

Each limb so perfect
Your expanse great love

Through it all
You stand so strong
Not expecting a thing
Except life's necessities

Oh wondrous tree
We have so much to learn from thee

Tonight I Will Come

I have a message for you to hear
So please come closer my dear
Let me whisper this in your ear

Tonight when I lay my head to sleep
As I get relaxed my inner self will glow
My eyes will start to spasm
My body start to twitch

With each breath
I will separate
Have no fear
With heart wide open
It's magical here

I lay there still
With power and will
Knowing I will see you tonight

Using all my might

I will see me at first sight

Sleeping so soundly

Like a baby

This is when I'll come for you

And when I do

We will fly above the clouds so new

I want to soar like never before

Hold you tight and show you a dance floor

One that doesn't compare

To anything we've ever dared

The night will be ours

Floating amongst the stars

As we float on the wings

Of what light and love brings

At the speed of light

We will see the galaxies

Earth beneath, we will be free

It's important to know

You must leave fear at the door
To fly so high
You must reach for the sky

Relax and breathe
Just let it be
It's a magical ride
We are sure to glide

Our spirits ignited
We are reunited

So when I go to sleep tonight
Know that I will come for you
To take you away from here
And visit all the galaxies in just one night

And when we return
With the light of the sun
You will know that
Tonight I will come

Why Not Have One More

Your eyes get wide
As you reach for what you see
There starts an energy
Others can see

Within feet of this thing
You simply gleam
To the world unseen
It sends out a beautiful ring

Your obsession for a dark chocolate covered
coffee bean

Like a ballet
One is swept across your lips
You almost seem to lose consciousness

Within seconds it melts
A flood of memories
Of childhood pleasures

It holds so many treasures

There is no doubt

It sends out such a beautiful ring

Your obsession for a dark chocolate covered
coffee bean

Tub

As I soak in a tub
Warm salty water soothing me
I think to myself
This is my reprieve

Reprieve from the anger
That roams this house
Free from the billowing doubts

It's so hard to stay steadfast and free
When you are around people who don't
believe
There lingering words of anger you see
Fill my head that I am unworthy

I come to the tub
To soak in the dark
To go to my place
I embark

As I delve deep
I think to myself
It's not me
It's them

I've pondered this question
More times than one
Is it a reflection?
What have I done?

But the more I try
The more I die
It simply seems
I must give in

Give in to my pleasures
And delve within
Love them forever
But grow new skin

As the tub water gets cold
I know the time has come

To be among the others

Aw what the heck
5 min more, til I open the door
Let me soak in this cold tub
Being with your warm glow

Taking A Moment

I take a moment
On a hot summers night
To step outside
And see your light

Quiet I lay
On the grass to gaze
At the stars above
I can feel the love

Naked are my eyes
Calm is my breath
I feel you close
I have to confess

Who would have known
This girl filled with such sadness
Would be here now
Overwhelmed with oneness

I am grateful to see

The Divine in me

As I lay quiet

May the world take time to see

Mirror

Good morning my love
Descending from above
All rested and renewed
Your body so nude

Your eyes filled with love
What did you dream of?
Can you remember what was shown you?
As dreams hold many clues

How did you sleep my beloved son?
Today I know we are one
So gentle so soft is your way
I am grateful to have you with me all day

Simply Divine

How can a simple touch from you
Do what it do?

Many a marvel
At this thing you do
Funny thing is
You're hardly in the room

Some question your ability
Simply because they don't see
But others believe
And they are the ones you relieve

You are a master of grace
Sometimes admittedly hard to face
For there are no secrets
When our body speaks

Each touch precise
Each manoeuvre just right

A map few know
Leaves clients aglow

Scents fill the room
Music conjures peace
As you float from spot to spot
It's all pretty neat

You challenge the norm
But you honor the sacred
Nothing can compare to your
Gentle guidance which awakens

You are simply Divine
Guiding the seekers to the sublime
Bodies once so halted
You recharge the defaulted

You open our hearts
You open our minds
With this thing called Bowen
We leave there feeling simply Divine

Let Love Rule

This connection we have
Is beyond imagination
For when in your presence
I resonate at a higher vibration

At first I questioned
And pondered is it lust?
Emotions and senses heightened
All would be a bust

Yet to call it lust
Would not be fair
As it is something with much more class and
flair

For it's something so special
That can only be called
Not an affair but unfair
An unfair of the soul

Maybe before we were brother and sis

I don't know but something pulls us in

It's hard to explain this feeling I have

But what I know is it's a wondrous thing

When we are apart the sum is still one

But I have to admit that it's less fun

To be with you sends my frequencies high

I have told you more than I can hide

When I feel your touch I know we are akin

When we connect there are no words

It's something so Divine

The secret to this unfair

Is we send energy each other's way

Not asking for a thing

Except an abundance of unconditional love
each day

Behind closed doors we uncover the clues

We know it's what binds and glues

This unfair of the soul

Sending us through another keyhole

The key to this unfair

Is to share our frequencies

So we can both grow and see

It a beautiful thing

This unfair

Sharing unconditional love

Of the Divine of we

I See You

My love
It pains me to see you hurt
So lost in the world of doubt

I am so grateful to have you
You make me feel so renewed
You make me see
All that I can be

You are a friend
We don't have to pretend
As I have been blessed with you
Brought to me to help me fend

When I struggle
You are there to pick me up
You are beyond Divine
Please never doubt

You have given me purpose

You have given me, me
How can someone be
So truly blessed with thee

You are one of gods creations
One on a journey of transformation
Not all will see the beauty in thee
But I do... I see you

Half Way There

On June 10th if you recall
I dowsed that I was to share them all
Seventy in total said they
It's hard to believe I'm half way

Each moment of the day
There are messages sent my way
If time allows
I write them down

It's hard to believe I've never before written like these
But something said, just let it be
Since then I've been amazed
At how easily they come
I know it must be from beyond

When you get hit with something so strong
You'll know because every dawn
You'll wake knowing what to do

Even if you don't believe in you

I am grateful for this gift
As it's given me a lift
I don't know how long it will last
But for now, I'm having a blast

I only hope that these messages to you
Will do what they are supposed to do
And someday we'll meet and
I can say, "Oh, it's you"

Until that day I will keep pen to paper
And enjoy this caper
In hopes that one day you'll see
We are all meant to be

Love Will Flow

There is a song
That proclaims
Love hurts
Let me explain

I would have to agree
For when you connect and finally open your heart
To the glories that be
It sets you free

Nothing can compare
It opens your 'eye' to what love is
And there is nothing above
This immortal bliss

I want to surround myself
With others who know
It will fill me and
Love will flow

Hook-y

What a beautiful day
To just be
It makes me what to play Hooky

I'd come to get you and take you to a place
Down by the lake without a trace
Where we could sit in the sun
Oh so far from the humdrum

I would put your hands in mine
Close our eyes to see
This wonderful energy
Between you and me

As energies flow
The chipmunks and birds
Would join in
Our spirits would be one
The outside; not in

And when the clock strikes four
It would be time to return
Return to a world
We've been before

Before the light and love
And all the glory above
We would hold the moment so dear
Walking our paths with no fear

There Are Always Answers

There are always answers to the questions
we weave

The signs there for us to see

The only thing we need

Is to Be in the right mind frame to see

When embracing your day

Remember to stay

Connected to your higher self

It's your new pulse

There are always answers you see

The important thing is to just let it be

The past and the future are not of concern

For it's something in this moment we must
learn

Look listen and feel the clues

You start to realize that even the blues

Are what make us learn who we truly are

And this my friend is what will make you a
star

Don't take in what the others may say
For you only have one purpose today
To listen to yourself and the many clues
Clues from the universe about you

There are always answers
To the questions we weave
Please my friends take the time
To be so that you may receive

Receive the insight
Of your plight
And know within
That it's your time to begin

Riding The Wave

Like the ocean so smooth
At times it must move
To replenish its nutrients
Like being born anew

This thing they call awakening
At times isn't an easy thing
You have to ride the waves
See truth; before grave

You may have your doubts
Disbelief may come in bouts
But in the end
You will be better than then

Moments filled with bliss
Some with despair
All there to help us
Help us repair

You have to ride the wave
Know you'll come out the other side
For as challenging as it is some days
It's so worth the ride

Why Can't I Look Into Your Eyes?

When you say the things you do
About what you see in me
Why can't I look into your eyes?
Is it because I don't believe?

When we are alone
And share our deepest thoughts
Why can't I look into your eyes?
Is it because I'm scared you'll find out?

It's obvious to me that what you see
Couldn't be me
No one has ever believed
So deeply in me

On the good day, I start believing
On the bad there is recoding
Why is it so hard for me?
To believe in me!

Practice Zone

Have you ever had a day
Of feeling so high
That when you look around
All you see is light reaching for the sky

Everything seems to have its own frequency
Everything interconnected by its energy

The trees have a glow
And do the birds know
Their tail winds are aglow

Everything it seems
Buildings, people and all things
Have a brilliance they show
Oh there is such beauty in how they all flow

On the days like this
I feel six feet tall, full of bliss
My feet firmly planted on the ground

With eyes in the clouds seeing all what is around

It's a miracle you see

Everything has an energy

Interconnected frequencies

There are no boundaries

This planet we roam

We call our home

But the truth of it is

It's simply a practice zone

Just Go In

This morning when I closed my eyes
To meditate and reach the skies
I get the sense I want to cry
When I feel you close – twitching eyes

A sense of warmth
Washes through me
A feeling of love
Beyond belief

I know your here
Watching over me
Please come in
I want to begin

It's been a few days
Since I've called you here
It seems I've been busy
Consumed with writing of you my dear
Just when I started feeling empty

Not knowing what to write
I decided I haven't taken
Time to take flight

So this morning I went
Deep within
And before you knew it
I knew where to begin

So if you find yourself
At a loss for what to do
My suggestion is
It's a perfect time to take for you

This morning when I closed my eyes
It held yet another surprise
Reminding me that during our busy lives
When there are moments we lose sight
It's important to take advantage of the
moment.... And just go in!

Did You See?

This morning was a change in routine

I had a doctor's appointment to follow up on
the sugar heed

So I boarded the subway at a different time
of day

And was shocked that I could hardly step in

As bodies filled the way

As I stepped and wiggled slowing on to the
car

I secured my spot

To the next station we go

Squished up to bodies I don't even know

It comes to mind the odd predicament I'm in

Surrounded by bodies that stay to their self

With each station we are in and out

Filling the car each time with new scouts

I ask myself as I scan around

How come you can't even look up and say

Hello, good day

Everyone with their fixed gaze

I scan a little more

In hopes to catch some eyes not fixed on the doors

But to my chagrin

Everyone it seems is closing in

Planning their route

To escape the predicament they are in

And rush off to their jobs

Can't be late for work again

Oh look it there

Someone just caught my eye

I smile and nod

And he politely gives in

Did you see?

He looked at me

And couldn't help but concede
That's all we need

Today I ask
When you rush from place to place
Remember that others are
Here to share this space

If we take the time
To recognize those souls
The result might blow your mind
So why not try and see what follows...

Epiphany

Epiphany they say
There always comes a day
When you gain insight
Today is it – my delight

Early I wrote
Awakening is no joke
Today I say
I think I've mastered the wave

Mindful of life's ups and downs
We always land with two feet on the ground
So knowing that now
Why not shoot for the clouds

Instead of following the wave
Day after day
Why not take a chance
Dive into the ocean at first glance

We are not here to follow

We are here to soar

Why do you think

There are opportunities galore

So go jump in the ocean

You have a notion

Of what it is your supposed to do

Get on with it – showing the greatness of
you

An ocean so deep

Filled with gentle souls

Majestic in nature

Singing sounds like gold

You are all these things

Go be the ocean baby

For all to see

Please!

My Heart Awoken On That Day

For the past seven years
I have hidden all my fears
Buried deep within me
Any need

When you hit me
It was simply what I needed
It was easy to let it be
For no one would know unless they see

Behind closed eyes
A lightning bolt appeared
At first I was naive
Thought I believed

But when I saw all you are
And felt your energy fill mine
I selfishly allowed
Because it was simply Divine

It's what I needed
It had been long since I was loved
It made me feel
Like it was so real and it was

As my heart awoken on that day
I shook from head to toe
Cramping every muscle
Almost painful as the frequency flowed

Pins and needles all over my face
Surprisingly not hard to embrace
For I knew the pain
Was for my gain

When it made my body shake
Like my body was on uptake
I pushed away my fear
And allowed more of you near

The ending result you see
Was a surprise to me

It was orgasmic

At first ashamed to say

I have never been touched that way

And I've had a few in my day

Light hearted and free

I can't explain how you came to me

But what I know

Is I will never be made love to like so

When you get hit with this you'll know

Nothing can compare to Divine flow

A secret lover to me

It's so hard not to be 24-7 to feel thee

But all I have to do

Is close my eyes

And I'm with you

No one wise

Thank you for letting me see

And be as one with thee

Thank you for awakening me

To a love so extreme

The Next Time I Close My Eyes

Last night when I meditated

I believe what most would say is I've graduated

Most won't believe me

But that's ok

Because until that walk in my soul

They won't have a clue

As I jump on the bed from the floor

I say my prayers

Giving gratitude and more

As I close my eyes

And fall to my special place

I can feel that slight breeze on my face

The tingling starts

My toes, back and head

As I lay on the bed

Deeper I go

Seeing colors of purple, white & gold

As adjustments are made

I can feel myself weighed

Each limb so heavy

Each muscle so relaxed

My body laying there untaxed

Each time I am alone

The shaking starts

But this time I feel so at home

Darts across my heart

As it begins, I can't help but call out

I want to go deeper, I blurt out

I want to be one; please fill me

And have you burn out all what is broken in me

My cheeks go blush

My body flushed

Vibrations get stronger
I think to myself how much longer

The next thing you know
I can feel this odd flow
A hand reaching in
From under the table
Caressing my skin

It's obvious to me
Since in the room I lay
With no one else to see
You have come to fill me

It's the hand of you
Why you are here
I don't know
Could it be you heard me, I let myself go

Moving across my internals
First my bladder so full
Feels like it's full of angel dust

Going pitter patter

Impulses sent
As angel dust extends
Twinkling all senses
Including my lentils

Trickling up my spine
I see you inside
Each touch an explosion
Is this the Divine?

My body gives in
As my legs and arms flail
You are obviously in
Hidden under my vail

Sending me into eruptions
I allow you to prevail
Excitement beyond measure
Oh what a pleasure

At moments disbelief

The tingling is even going out my feet

Almost lost in this bliss

All of sudden my stomach muscles skip

Like being tickled by a thousand feathers

My body erupts in spontaneous glitter

Laughter grows

From where I don't know

But laying there half clothed

I feel my body giving in

Filled with ecstasy

Beyond imaginable fantasy

Laughing won't cease

So I scream out – I can't take anymore right now please

Never before

Have I had such laughter

Sounding like a sniffling child

From my belly so wild

As I open my eyes
How do I confess?
The next thing you know
She comes through the door

Without hesitation
I explain your visitation
I should be embarrassed
But instead I wasn't the slightest

With a skip in my step
I quickly get redressed
Wondering if it shows
This Divine glow

I wonder to myself
Will I see you inside?
The next time
I close my eyes

Can't Have It Both Ways

Today I struggle
As last night you see
I had what I'll call a spiritual awakening

It was an amazing trip
But the problem you see
Is today it totally consumes me

I'm finding it hard
To concentrate of late
My body excited
Every cubic inch of me awake

This feeling I have
I have not had for some time
Because you see
I have been celibate body and mind

It's hard to exist
In my daily routine

I feel all I want
Is to be unseen

I tell myself
You have work to do
Come on girl
Get a grip on you

But then without reason
My body sends me into treason
As much as I loved the act
I need to get my body back

It's affecting my thoughts
And I need to stop
So I can get my work done
And choose a time and place for this
freedom

I guess you can't have it both ways
You get what you ask for
So the only thing I can do today

Is get my work done and run out the door

I look forward to the time
When there are no pressures of time
And I can simply meet you inside
And without fear be with my Divine

When You Fear

When you fear
Remember I am near
Take a moment to open your heart
I will be there in a dart

Ask not to protect you
But to cleanse away the fear
This is when I will come, my dear
And channel the strength through

Ask not for the problems to be solved
As they are a lesson for your resolve
Simply go within to see
I'll guide you to a different place to be

Once fear is squashed
Your perspective cleansed and washed
You will see again
Where you must begin

When You Hurt Inside

When your anger takes over
I use to aim for cover
But with each day I get stronger now
So instead I try to calm you down

You see the demon in you
Takes over as you morph into two
I see it in your eyes
Everything you despise

As I remind you to breath
And say remember it's me
I am not the enemy
Honey, it's me

Please don't get lost
In your bitterness and loss
You are making yourself sick
With all these antics

If you could just stop and see
Come closer and just be with me
We can talk it through
And find the real you

For a moment you stopped
Your inner hurtful thoughts
And I could see you come back
But then a setback

You're replaying the events
Saying it helps when you vent
But if you could just see
It's sending you back into misery

As the moments transpire
I am able to inspire
Enough were you can
Face the world again

Come with me and believe
If we try again, we can achieve

As your defences shut down
And you start to feel the ground

My heart is warmed
And I am in love again
Fully compassionate
And I have your back

Don't you see?
When you hurt inside
It hurts me
I will always be by your side

Please remember to stay
In this healthy way
As it brings the beauty
In each our days

A Simple Act

A simple act of kindness
Can make some ones day
A simple gesture
Can make someone light the way

A simple act of love
Can fill someone with Joy
A simple act of compassion
Can fill someone with Hope

A simple step towards togetherness
Can change the world you see
A simple step towards humbleness
Can change our universe for thee

A simple act for us to be
The actor or actress as the lead
A simple thought you see
It's up to you and me

Beauty

The beauty that surrounds us
Always amazes me
From the beauty of a leaf
Trembling in the breeze

To the softness of the grass
Under my feet
To the beauty of an ass
Or Don-kee

Surrounded by all this beauty
How can someone not pause to see?
There is beauty all around us
Take a look and see

If you pause and look up
You may even notice an eagle souring high
Souring the sky
Taking your prayers away making them
alive

Pause and give a listen
What do you hear?
Nothing you say
Isn't that heaven my dear?

Look at the sun
And the brilliance it shines
Look at that ray breaking through the clouds
It's a stairway calling out loud

Look at the moon
Can you see the energy it has?
For in the midst of darkness
It can light a path

Do you see the drop of rain?
For it falls so gently in the terrain
It resonates all around
Travelling through the ground

Do you see how people move?

Like a nucleus so smooth
The beauty of electrons bombarding
Causing a chain reaction in unison

There is beauty all around
All you have to do is take your spot
And look around
Why not give it a shot?

I See I

Today you're more at peace
I feel a sense of relief
You blessed me with your smile
It's been a while

Then you said with a lift
I see you
What a gift
I reply, I see you

As I scan around
The dog lying down
I look her way and say
I see you too

The birds as they fly bye
I think to myself
I see you too

What a gift
A few simple words
From their lips
Can bring peace to this world

Thank you Universe
For this overflowing purse
Of life's simplest pleasures
All beyond measure

I look back and catch your eye
The old feeling back
One cannot deny
I see you... I see I

Fear Wins

Oh sweetheart

When will you see?

This bitterness and anger

Doesn't become thee

I remind you to breathe

And your next breath you talk about her again

I tell you she's not worth it but I am

Please don't get lost

In your ego so blind

Open up your mind

And see your beauty within

The others who make comments again

Just ignore and pray for them

You see it is how you perceive

You need to close your eyes and believe

I had that spark today
But I can't keep living this play
For it's filled with coldness and anger
It's seeping back in our way

I've asked my angels to clear your fear
For I see fear is winning again
Please baby come back down here
And don't let it win, don't bargain

Clear that fear
So that you can find the time to breathe
Breathe in the love that sits across the way
Breathe in the beauty from within
Please baby, please before the fear wins

I've Had Enough

I've had enough I scream
Almost feels like a dream
I put my hands to my ears
"I can't take this anymore" I squeal

I sit there for minutes
Trying to drown the sound of your critics
How is it you can't see?
It's killing me

My energy is drained
I cannot withstand
This state of mind
You continue to bandstand

I see you there inside
But I don't recognize your mask
Burning you up inside
I have failed my task

I know it's not up to me to make you see

But I guess I just hope you could level up
with me

It seems we are on different paths

I simply don't know if I should stand here –
as life goes bye too fast

Caught In Your Web

Caught in your web
Of internal lies
You remind me
This is who I wed

It resonates with me today
And I think is this the same
Woman who stands before me on this day

Well of course it is
The same soul within
But the thing that's not
Is her anger and rot within

I ask myself how long do I hold your hand?
I made a commitment more that 14 years
ago
But today if chances are you will continue to
get lost in this war
Then how can I stay as it's killing me

I picture then that I've moved on

Knowing now that you can fend for most

But then I think how it will look

People will say... see she is afloat

Meaning I know you have good days and bad

And some of life's circumstances have been sad

But I have always supported you

And I guess I don't want people to think less of you

So do I stay simply to keep away the thieves?

If I leave right now I know you will grieve

That doesn't help with therapy

So for now I must retain my reprieve

I find a place to go within

And they tell me I'm on the right track again

The angels say they have heard my call

And that the plans are in place to win it all

So I have to trust that for now I stay

And that things will be better some day

I just hope that my strength and will

Will cradle me to til the morning light shines
through the window sill

I Want

I want sunny days ahead

Where we laugh and play

New learnings fill our head

And wonder where went the day

I want to make new discoveries

Trudging new paths of fantasies

Laying in the clover

And gazing at what's over

I want to hold your hand

And have sparks go off like the theatrics of a
rock band

I want to stare your way

And have it fill me for days

I want to touch you and feel the softness of
your skin

And follow each crease and then retrace
where I've been

I want moments when we are in our own
happy places

Knowing each is there by the look on our
faces

I want what was and no longer is

It pains me to think all you want is this

This stagnant life where all is a fight

I just wish you could see your light

I don't know if and when you'll see

But for now, it's exhausting me

I feel I should hang on for you

But someday I will have to take care of me
too

Some Day

As I sit here and feel my stomach heave
I realize what I really want is to be
Be alone somewhere far away
Somewhere where no one knows my name

Fill my day with no responsibility
Other than being of service to thee
Just imagine the possibilities
Me totally here for my higher good, I
believe

I believe one day it will come crashing in
For I can feel it building within
It doesn't take away what we have had
It simply means I'm growing

Some day you will see
That it's best for both you and me
And when we cross our paths again

Hopefully the time has made you look
within

For now I want to be left alone

Time to remind me of my solemn oath

Where I can breathe the sweet smelling air

And sit in silence lost in the nature

What I really want

Is to be lost someday

Where no one knows me

And just let's me be

I can then follow through with all urges

For now I sit with the feeling to purge

I don't love you any less

I simply need more I confess

Why Do I Stay?

My body scrapped and bruised
Why do I continue to take the abuse?
I am tired and worn
My mind torn

I do it all too simply satisfy you
I don't even want a thank you
But what I get frustrated at
Is the fact that you have already lined up the next act

Job after job
I feel robbed
Like a work hand
Jumping at every twist of your magic wand

I have a busy week and need to rest
But you've seemed to rob me of my best
My mind is playing tricks on me
Saying I am here to be of service to thee

But I now know there is a greater thee

One whom service fills me with glee

So why do I stay and continue the cycle

For after this job there will be another one
that will cripple

The cycle seems to never end

No matter what messages I send

I don't even think you care

For if I resist you glare

As you run upstairs to play your game

You say you've run a hot bath for me

Like it's supposed to wash away

All the sadness that is coming off me

I lay in the tub after serving your dinner

And all I hear is your game comments bitter

There's no life left here

I am so saddened my dear

Why do I stay?
In my head I say there will come a day
When I love myself more
And will walk out this door

But for now I lay in the tub
Something I have now been accustomed too
To get some space and retrace
Why I do the things I do

Someday I will soak
And finally feel broke
And cry out all this sadness
Making me see clearly this is madness

But for now I enjoy the comfort of me
And close my eyes to find the Divine in me
Oh angels please comfort me
And tell me where I'm supposed to be

Message To My Friend

As I hold a small geode of Amethyst
I am sending you all my best
For a day of strengthened intellect
And a mind at rest

As I envision a wash of while flow
Going over my head to my toes
I bring you in
Asking for calmness, clarity and its energy
to cleanse

May anxiety be dissolved
And the day's problems resolved
Leaving only optimism and a grace
That fills each moment and space

May I be a channel of hot grace for thee
And send my soul sista energy
So her day can flow as light as a feather

Not a worry in the world... Not even the
weather

As I hold this geode of Amethyst in my
hand

This is all I wish for my friend

Please send her a healthy dose

And let her know I am close

It Could Just Be

It could just be

That this whole process of writing is for me

But something in my gut tells me

That I still believe they are as much for you,
as they are for me

Never before have I been so consumed

It fills my thoughts, my day - writing
feverishly at noon

When I speak I catch myself talking in
rhyme

It's been a ride, simply Divine

It's not for me to question

But simply be

And see where this is all taking me

For at the end, I do not know

If this is all I am to show

But if and when I receive the next task

I will gladly throw up my hands and let it fill
my flask

For you see

This task has been as much for you

As it was for me

Learning more about the authentic me

Do You Ever Get Tired?

Do you ever get tired
Of taking care of everyone else?

On the days you need your rest
You are there for them with a smile
Showing off your best

On the days you need to be alone
You are there for them
Helping them get their work done

On the days you need to get some space
You are there for them
Not complaining, full of grace

On the days you need to get your work done
You are there for them
Trying to make their day more fun

How is it that you are always there?

Do you ever get tired?

And feel like skipping through the air

Or throwing your hands up, would you dare?

Please tell me how you do what you do

I need to learn to be so much more like you

Through thick and thin you are always there

How is it that you don't give in, instead you
grin and bear

Like a Flower

Like a flower we all grow at different rates

Some of us naturally grow abundance great

Some of us still beautiful in their own right

But need some nurturing and love to reach
for the light

Each started from the same seed

Some given more opportunities

But there is beauty in all

Each having their different call

Some bloom in direct light

While others grow in darkness to be just
right

Some crawl sprouting seeds to continue the
fight

Others grab on to reach greatness – their
showing so bright

Some grow fast

While others relax

Some drop new seeds their god given duty

But all in all they have purpose and beauty

So today be sure to take the time to go smell one

Let it tickle your senses and fill your lungs

Let it remind you of your beauty

As we are all one

It Will Be So

I have always believed
In a power greater than me
Else why would it be
That deceased family members I see

As a child I knew
The mind was a powerful thing
For if I envisioned it
It would be

I remember once
My mother so pleased
Came home
With a present for me

It was a beautiful bathing suit
Which sported wonderful colours to boot
Like a Hawaiian lai
Displayed with flowers and leaves, would
make my day

The disappointment came

When I went to try it on

It wouldn't go past my hips

No matter how much tanning lotion I put on

I quickly took the tag

The suit donned

Which included a picture

Of a model so bronzed

I imagined myself as she

And each day it was a ritual to me

To my father's disbelief sporting a grin

Without changing diet, I was thin

I loved that bathing suit for years on end

Never wanting to give up on it

For it meant

I had made something materialize

Simply by imaging myself as she

I was thin and with my eyes

I could see the picture was me

So the lesson here is if you want it so
You must have a clear picture and know
The more you feel it is already true
The more of what you want in life will come
to you

I know it's true
Because it happened to me
And I had a witness
My father who believed

You see if you really want something
All you have to do
Is get a clear vision
Believe and it will be so

Sent Me For A Loop

This afternoon when you contacted me
I have to admit as the pit of my stomach fell
I felt like dropping to my knees

Again I thought I can't handle any more
Will tonight be the night I walk out the door?
But again everything is telling me to stay
Until September and then will come the day

I have to ask myself why you would do what you do
I've always thought a partnership warranted a decision by two
I can see you wanting your independence
But for heaven's sake not when it involves a new household expense

It seems you can never just be
You must always have something to give you false glee

No thought or consideration for others

And if someone needs, you take cover

I can't believe this is who you are

I guess I have always seen it but chose to look from afar

Never did I think that when we had a solid plan

That you would renege and start to bargain

Bargain with our future like it grows on trees

For something that could have been free

Your motive I can't comprehend

Are you trying to cause an end?

Maybe I'm blind and it's all you're wishing for

Wish I knew so we could just get on with it and close this door

For now I'll let you rant

Because I know you will when tonight I vent

Today you sent me for a loop

Can't wait to hear the whole scoop

Time will tell

If you still have me under your spell

Could It Be

Could it be you?
Who's walking bye
As we catch each other's eyes
Could it be you who sees?

Could it be you?
The guy studying for his exam
With his head in his hand
Could it be you who sees?

Could it be you?
The pregnant woman resting her head
Could it be you who sees?
We are all connected and believes

Could it be you?
The young girl on the phone
Could it be you who sees?
We are all on but frequencies

Could it be you?

The janitor pushing the broom

Could it be you who sees?

We are in here in our playroom

It could be you who sees

And knows I AM here

It is you I see

Another piece of this universal energy

Rain

It nurtures all what grows
In distant rivers it flows
From high in the sky
Making everything wet which was dry

As it comes down on me
I look up and embrace each
Each droplet so cool and wet
For it falls from where molecules met

As I stand exposed
But fully clothed
I murmur, wash over me
And cleanse all around with thee

Cleanse the past that was
And the future that will
I'm taking this moment to connect above
For it's a moment to be still

At this point in time
I am not the only one touched by this Divine
The guy over there with his wet soaked hair
At this moment in time it has made us a pair

Is it Divine intervention?
To make everyone stop with clear intention
To look around and soak in
All the Divine which lies within

It Amazes Me

According to Freud, we are born with an ID
And this ID is important to our personality
It allows us to get our basic needs
Based on what heightened or excites thee

The amazing thing you see
Is this ID doesn't care about anything in reality
Other than its own needs
Like an in built committee

The hardest part I believe
Is knowing if it is the ID we hear
Or is it the I AM, masked by my fear?

Pain And Suffering

Pain and suffering are in our lives in many different ways

The death of a loved one, family troubles, or illnesses can fill our day

Pain and suffering comes in many forms

But don't forget who you are for there is hope, strength, love and more

When you're feeling blue

Know that there is a truth

Happiness and love can be yours for the taking

All you have to do is ask your angels for an awakening

The greatest challenge is

To have the strength within

During your darkest days

When you think there is no way to win

For if you stop and ask for help while looking Deep within

You may just be surprised at who comes knocking

During times of struggle your angels are always near

You simply need to recognize that and surrender your fear

For the journey you will travel will change you for life

Believe me when I say

Your angels are near

They will show you the light

No matter who you are

Or what you do

Know the Saints, Gods and angels are there for you

They have a play, you need not know

Just have faith and let it be so

Recognize these wonderful gifts in our lives

As they are what will make you feel alive

In Order To Grow

In order to grow
I must face it and know
That what I fear the most
Is like a parasite and host

I say I want to love me
But refuse to face all that binds me
Seems simpler then
To just give in

The ego is a powerful thing
That sometimes makes this life not worth living
But you must fight
For if you do, you will see the light

To think it's easier to go home now
Would simply mean you would have to come back down

All that you have learnt in another body
rebirthed

So don't give up now, you are too close

Know this is all the plan

Tomorrow you will feel strong again

Remember the love beyond measure

Buried deep is that treasure

Hold yourself tight

For the ride will bring delight

Love yourself for what you are

And baby I promise you the stars

###

Closing Thoughts

A year ago I was told I may never be able to work again. Wow, what an amazing Journey I've had since those words were first spoken to me. I know I have a long way to go to being forever healed but that's ok because I know I'm not alone now. I have been touched by the Divine and each day, grow stronger. Yes of course I still have low days as you can see from some of the poems but hey without those days I wouldn't be able to recognize the amazing ones. I am starting to love myself more each day and the people around me have a choice. They can love me for who I AM today and reap the benefits of my love or they can choose to fear the real me. Their choice, not mine! I don't know what lies ahead but I don't need to know.

All I need to do is enjoy the moment, enjoy the ride of finding me. I wouldn't change a thing for a million dollars. I now know that I am blessed (we are all blessed); we just need to open our eyes, open our hearts and believe. I challenge each and every one out there to find the real you, if we all could take the time - make an investment in ourselves and believe you are a brilliant spiritual being, can you imagine what this world might look like! Hmmmm, I'm seeing lots of red - hearts that is! I believe, do you?

Connect with Me Online:

Twitter:
http://twitter.com/#!/mafia_sweets

Facebook:
https://www.facebook.com/pages/Do-You-Believe/260797250617958#!/pages/Do-You-Believe/260797250617958?sk=wall

www.ingramcontent.com/pod-product-compliance
Lightning Source LLC
Chambersburg PA
CBHW060038040426
42331CB00032B/1014